The Story of Clapham Common

GW00778117

published by

THE CLAPHAM SOCIETY

ABOUT THE CLAPHAM SOCIETY

The Society's objects include safeguarding the character of Clapham Common and the protection and enhancement of features of historic interest or public amenity in Clapham. Founded in 1963, it now has over 500 members. We aim to strengthen Clapham's identity and sense of community.

The Clapham Society is an entirely non-political organisation and a registered charity; it is affiliated to the Civic Trust.

Our Activities include:

Meetings on topics of local interest and concern. An example is our public meeting in January 1995 about the Parking Scheme, which helped to persuade councillors to drop this badly prepared plan.

The Local Community. The Clapham Society is working with local traders to revitalise Clapham High Street. We helped to organise a fund-raising event for the PC Patrick Dunne Memorial Fund.

Social Events.   The opportunity to meet other members at parties and informal meetings, often held in one of Clapham's interesting old buildings.

Planning.   The Planning Sub-Committee draws on a wealth of experience and professional expertise and its comments carry weight with the borough councils. The Society has often given evidence at public enquiries into controversial development plans.

The Society is taking a keen interest in development plans for the Bus Garage and South London Hospital sites.

Newsletters, approximately monthly, keep members informed of local issues and Society events.

Publications. The Clapham Society has published several high quality books on the history of Clapham, its buildings and inhabitants. We produce cards of Clapham views by artists past and present.

Clapham Common

One of the Society's most important rôles is to act as a guardian for the Common, Clapham's most precious asset. The Society aims to represent all users of the Common, part of which lies within the Borough of Wandsworth, working to conserve it as an open space.

We highlighted the threat to it from the Red Route proposals. We are fighting for a Code of Practice to improve the management of events on the Common, with a ban on those whose scale makes them inappropriate for this location. The Clapham Society supports the use of the Common for sport whilst preserving its character.

Our Tree Fund has replaced trees lost in the 1987 hurricane.

A long-running campaign against parking on Common land led to a ruling by the local Ombudsman in our favour; problems of this nature, though, continue.

———————

If you are interested in Clapham and concerned to protect and enhance its character, and would like to be part of a friendly local group, you should —

Join the Clapham Society

A membership application form with details of subscription rates is overleaf.

Data Protection Act 1984: please indicate if you object to your membership details being computerised.

Registered Charity No. 279595.

Application for Membership

Please complete this form and send it to the Hon. Membership Secretary:

Mrs Joyce Luck
15 Cavendish Road
London SW12 0BH

I/We wish to join the Clapham Society.

Name ....
(Please print)

Address ....

....

....

Postcode ....

Annual Subscriptions

(Please tick the appropriate category)

- ❑ Ordinary membership.................£4.00
- ❑ Each additional member from
  the same household...................£2.00
- ❑ Persons of pensionable age..........£2.00
- ❑ Business members....................£15.00

Members living outside Clapham are asked to pay £2.50 extra to cover postage.

We would prefer you to pay by Standing Order, completing the form opposite. If you prefer not to pay this way, please enclose your first subscription by cheque or postal order.

Banker's Order

To ....Bank

....Branch

Address..

....

....

Please pay the sum of £ .... immediately, and thereafter annually on 10 April, until this order is cancelled, to:

National Westminster Bank PLC
Clapham Common Branch
P.O. Box 3059
London SW4 7SN
(Sorting Code 60-05-34)

for the credit of the Clapham Society,
(Account No. 22217045)

Name..

Address...

....

....

Account No. | | | | | | | | |

Signature ....

Date...

The Membership Secretary will forward this form to your bank.

CONTENTS

Front cover. Clapham Common showing the bandstand and refreshment house; watercolour specially commissioned for this book from Christina Bonnett

1. The Spring Well by T.M. Baynes (detail); the well, on the north side of the Common, was built by public subscription in 1825 to replace an earlier well nearby which was inadequate

INTRODUCTION

THE CLAPHAM SOCIETY was formed over 30 years ago to be the civic amenity society for Clapham. The preservation of Clapham Common as a priceless urban amenity has always been one of the Society's principal concerns.

In this book we have tried to give a vivid idea through words and pictures of the changing nature of the Common from medieval times to the present day. Our wider purpose is to interest the reader in the preservation of the Common as a much-needed lung of fresh air amidst the ever-increasing pressure of traffic pollution.

We have used the Common's history to illustrate its special importance to Clapham's inhabitants down the years as they have fought for its preservation.

The Clapham Society follows a long tradition among local residents, first formalised in 1768 in the residents' committee, of providing a voice for local concern in the face of the depredations which have threatened the green space. These have included enclosure, neglect, tree disease, personal safety and storms. In the 20th century noise and air pollution, and environmental and ecological decay have added to the problems.

The purpose of the public space – whether park or common – has been described as a "centre of civility and common terrain that allows urban strangers to drop their guard in a pocket of nature that is held in trust for everybody."

Clapham Common, as its name suggests, is a common, not a park. The Common has little landscaping and no flower beds such as are found in municipal parks. There are no enclosed areas except for council depots, children's playgrounds, and certain sports facilities such as tennis, bowls and netball. It is open all night and there are no park-keeper patrols. For practical purposes it is largely a recreational area. There is a long tradition of using the Common for a wide range of sporting activities – one of the most successful aspects of the Common today as many local sportsmen and women know.

Clapham Common lay partly within the parish of Clapham and partly within Battersea. Thus today it is divided between the boroughs of Lambeth and Wandsworth. Management of the Common, however, is wholly the responsibility of Lambeth (with Wandsworth looking after Tooting Bec Common, which also straddles the two boroughs). Meeting the demands of different users in a difficult financial climate is a challenging task. The Society believes that it is vital to continue to aim for the objectives outlined in the opening paragraph.

The involvement of local schools and voluntary bodies in nature conservation needs to be encouraged. The balance of the needs of sport and the ecology of the Common must be kept in harmony to accommodate conservation of the past and provision for the future. We hope that this book will remind us all of the heritage our Common represents so that we can begin to work together to give the lie to its description as the biggest traffic island in Europe.

The earliest history of the Common itself has been

documented entirely from archeological excavation. A dig in the 1980s recovered prehistoric hand axes, bowls, flints, and pottery dating from the Iron Age.

Clappeham, or Clopham, is the Old English name for a village, homestead or enclosure on a hill. The earliest reference to Clappeham is in the register of Chertsey Abbey (sited at Tooting). In the time of King Alfred (late 9th century), a Saxon nobleman named Aelfrid is recorded as giving a large area of land in the manor of Clappeham to his wife.

Another reference is to Osgood Clapha (*left*), who was a standard bearer of the Danish King Hardicanute. It was at a ceremony to celebrate the wedding of Osgood's daughter that King Hardicanute died suddenly in June 1042, thus enabling Edward the Confessor to return from exile in Normandy to be crowned King of England.

Moira Leech
Chairman,
The Clapham Society

2. Osgood Clapha – *engraving by Mary G. Houston from* Old and New Clapham *(1903)*

5

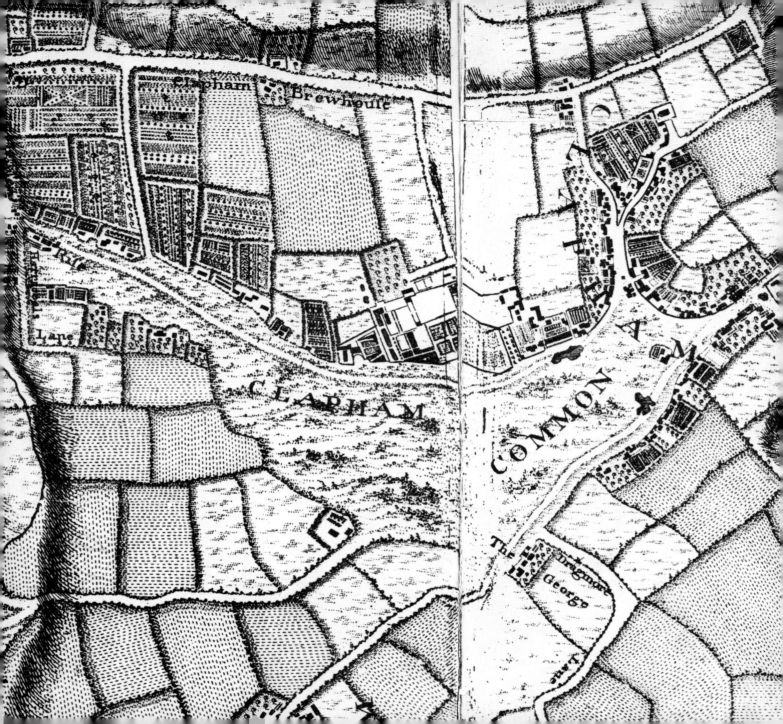

Clapham Brewheuse

CLAPHAM

COMMON

Hill ...

Lane

The Drigmore George

EARLIEST DAYS

FROM THE TIME of the Domesday survey in 1086, the wooded but uncultivated ground of the Common was split between the manors of Battersea to the west and Clapham to the east. Although owned by the two Lords of the Manor, the locals used it as pasture for animals and as a source of firewood and water. By 1326 the Clapham estate was said to consist of "a capital messuage [a dwelling house with adjoining buildings and land], 254 acres and a quarter of arable land, 20 of meadow, 140 of underwood, 6 of pasture, rents of assize of free tenants and bondmen ... three cocks and a hen". Clapham's first free-range poultry!

It was the topography that made Clapham an ideal place in which to settle. It was the first high ground above the Thames' flood plain to the south of London. The 220 acres of grass and woodland lie on a plateau formed by a layer of gravel overlying clay. This soil profile allows a reservoir of clean water to build up in the impervious clay.

*3. **Map of the County of Surrey** (detail) by John Rocque, 1745 – one of the first maps of the area*

*4. **Pepys at the Plough** by J. Priestman Atkinson, from* Old and New Clapham *(1903)*

John Rocque's map of the County of Surrey in 1745 shows Clapham as a typical rural hamlet. The underlying street pattern established in the medieval period also remains unchanged on the Rocque map. The road to the north of the village, now known as the Wandsworth Road, was the main route to Kingston and the rest of Surrey. The London Road, now known as South Side, is thought to follow the route of Stane Street, the old Roman road.

In the 18th century, the Common was flanked by fields and a variety of renowned hostelries or inns, such as the The Plough (*above*). The first reference to "The Pavement" appears at this time – "skirting the fringes of the Common" near to the village.

7

LORDS OF THE MANOR

5. View on Clapham Common (detail) by J.M.W. Turner, c.1800-1805; mentioned by John Ruskin in 1856 as being unfinished, this painting formed part of Turner's bequest to the nation

ALTHOUGH THE LORD of the Manor of Battersea had been an ardent Royalist during the English Civil War, the villagers of Clapham, loyal to their own lord, were staunch supporters of Cromwell's Parliamentarians. This may have been the origin of the animosity between the two manors over their shared rights of the Common.

The settlement of Clapham was situated in the area around St. Paul's Church and Old Town until the late 18th century. The Common was only a peripheral part of the territory of Battersea Manor. The main centre of Battersea was around Battersea Square, where the church and the manor house were situated. The manor also contained the estates of Battersea Fields and part of Wandsworth Common.

However, tensions grew between the parishioners of Clapham and Battersea over grazing rights. Battersea claimed rights to almost half the Common, and in 1716 the Battersea parishioners erected a bank and ditch along the boundary line separating Clapham Common from what was then called Battersea East Common: the Clapham parishioners promptly filled the ditch!

The Common was in a deplorable state, overgrown with gorse and furze, and travellers negotiating its boggy, bumpy roads also had to contend with lurking highwaymen. Robert Forrester, who robbed travellers on the highway between London and Clapham dressed in a night-gown, admitted to being "a notorious sinner, addicted to evil company, lying, uncleanness and pride ... drinking and other vices."

Another favourite pastime on the Common was the killing of hedgehogs. This poor man's blood sport totalled a "bag" between 1718 and 1732 of 84 hedgehogs and 19 polecats. From contemporary paintings, it appears there was the additional pleasure of a duck-shoot on the Common!

In the 17th century the most splendid house in the Clapham parish was on North Side near to where Trinity Hospice now

stands. This property was on Sir Dennis Gauden's estate overlooking the Common. Samuel Pepys, the diarist, visiting him in July 1663, wrote: "When I came there the first thing was to show me his house, which is almost built. I find it very regular and finely contrived, and the gardens and offices about it as convenient as ever I saw in my life. It is true he hath been censured for laying out so much money."

Pepys' friend, William Hewer bought the house and

6. View from the Nine Elms on Clapham Common by J. Powell, c.1825; Mount Pond is on the right, the Nine Elms on the left

Pepys later joined him there. His fellow diarist John Evelyn teasingly referred to it as "your Paradisian Clapham". Pepys died at this house in 1703.

9

WEALTHY RESIDENTS

BY THE MID-1700s Clapham and its Common were within easy reach of the city of London and grand residences were being built around the green space. There are accounts of Sir Thomas Hankey and his lady, new and wealthy residents of Clapham, being victims of a highwayman on the Common in 1751. In 1761 Captain Freeman of the Buckinghamshire militia shot a highwayman who attempted to rob him on the Common.

The religious life of Clapham had centred on the old parish church in the village which stood on the site of the present St. Paul's Church. By the 1750s the old church was badly in need of repair, as well as being too small for the growing population of Clapham. Although it took nearly 20 years for the Church Committee to reach a decision, the new church was finally planned and built on the Common. Under the terms of the will of Sir Richard Atkins, owner of the Clapham manor,

7. Holy Trinity Church engraved by B. Hewlett, 1795; the church, completed in 1776, is shown here with its original porch, before the extension in 1812

an Act of Parliament was required to transfer ownership of part of the family property.

By 1776 the present Holy Trinity Church, designed by Kenton Couse, was built. Couse, a pupil of Henry Flitcroft, had redesigned the frontage of 10 Downing Street, ten years earlier.

The new residents viewed the Common as an attractive backdrop to their fine properties. Encroachment on to the Common had already begun with the fencing of the Mount Pond and the Thornton family had built their stables on the Common, on the area now known as Rookery Road. The residents also made efforts to beautify the area – planting new trees, draining and levelling and improving some of the roads.

Charles Baldwin, a local magistrate, who lived at the Grange on the west side of the Common, began maintenance work in 1722, funded in part out of his own pocket and in part from public subscription. By 1760, thanks to the regular contributions of local residents, the Common was well planted with trees of various species.

THE MOUNT POND

M OUNT POND, with its central island, probably originated as a gravel pit for the building of the turnpike road to Tooting. Encroachment of the Common reached its apogee in 1746 when a banker, Mr Henton Brown, sought permission from the parish vestry to fence the Mount Pond. The vestry refused, but the Lord of the Manor granted permission for Mr Brown to pipe water from the pond to his house on South Side. Mr Brown then built a bridge and a pagoda-summer house on the Mount and with his small boat moored alongside, he no doubt believed it to be an extension of his estate! He was granted an expensive 20-year lease and was also required to pay five shillings to the poor of the parish for this privilege.

When in 1768 a Mr Fawkes tried digging a trench 50 metres long on the Common, the other inhabitants objected and set up a committee to maintain the rights and privileges of the parishioners. The committee sought to protect the Common, directing that dung hills be removed and the opening of gravel pits and lopping of trees be restricted. The edges of the ponds and gravel pits were to be sloped off. Broom and ornamental trees were planted, and elms were added to the south and west of the newly built Holy Trinity Church.

Benjamin Franklin, the American scientist and statesman, used Mount Pond for his early experiment in pouring oil on troubled water. He used to stay with the West India merchant Christopher Baldwin, who had a fine house on West Side. Franklin wrote : "Think for a moment of the pleasure we had in smoothing the ruffled surface of the pond on our Common between me and neighbour Brown."

Another more eccentric scientist, Henry Cavendish (1731-1810), later bought Henton Brown's house, and this reclusive grandson of the 2nd Duke of Devonshire turned the entire house into a giant laboratory, where he conducted experiments to determine the density of the Earth.

8. The Mount, Clapham Common by T.M. Baynes, lithograph published in 1827; now known as Mount Pond, it is one of the four surviving ponds on the Common

LIFE ON THE COMMON

ALTHOUGH STILL OWNED by the Lords of the Manors of Clapham and Battersea, and used in places as an extension to their properties by the surrounding householders, to the ordinary people of Clapham, the Common was still a source of water, firewood and pasture for their livestock. On windy days it was also a drying field (*below*). It was normal practice for people to hang their washing out to dry on the Common – although they were discouraged by the church beadle from hanging clothes on the church fence.

The Common was used for archery in the early 18th century and for horse racing since 1674. Horse riding was banned, however, because it was deemed to be damaging to the turf. Despite a petition of 5,500 names, the banning decision was not overturned. The only riding allowed on the Common was on a specially created turf gallop along the road leading from Balham to Battersea Rise, which survives to this day as The Avenue.

9. Hanging out washing to dry on the Common, as drawn by J. Powell in the 1820s

10. *The Hopping Match* on Clapham Common, 1827; Jackson *"exhibiting his agility"*

Fairs were popular, but were considered a nuisance by some and were restricted to Easter, Whit and Derby Day by the 1780s. Events such as bare-knuckle boxing matches were allowed and the sketch of a hopping match (*above*), by an unidentified artist, depicts the boxer John Jackson, champion of England between 1795 and 1803, "exhibiting his agility". In a match against the mighty brewer, George Inglestone, Jackson, having broken his right leg, offered to continue the battle with the damaged leg tied to a chair.

Jackson ran a famous boxing school in Bond Street which was patronised by the aristocracy, including Byron, who wrote in *Hints from Horace*:

"And men unpractised in exchanging knocks
Must go to Jackson ere they dare to box."

15

THE CLAPHAM SECT

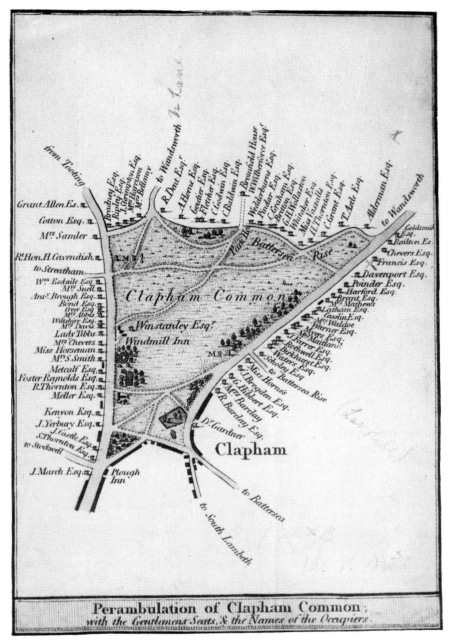

Perambulation of Clapham Common; with the Gentlemens Seats, & the Names of the Occupiers.

BY THE LATE EIGHTEENTH CENTURY, besides wealthy city men such as John Hatchard, founder of the Piccadilly booksellers, a group of social reformers, known as the Clapham Sect, had begun to take up residence around the Common.

The philanthropist Zacharay Macaulay (1768-1838) was one of the founders of the Sect, which was noted for its religious principles and reforming zeal. Macaulay had been horrified by the conditions of black workers on the Jamaican plantations and later, as Governor of Sierra Leone in West Africa, did much to help the slave workers and even took passage on a slave ship to observe their conditions for himself. On his return from Africa, he brought with him 25 children, setting up the African Academy in Clapham to give them a Christian education. Unfortunately, some children died, probably because of exposure to the cold and to diseases foreign to them.

11. Perambulation of Clapham Common, from C. Smith's Actual Survey of the Road from London to Brighthelmston, c.1800

12. *Henry Thornton* (1760-1815) *by John Hoppner*

to his life-long friend Henry Thornton (1760-1815).

Thornton (*left*) was born in Clapham, the third generation to live here. Henry and his father John were both members of the Clapham Sect.

The son of Zacharay Macaulay, Thomas Babington Macaulay (1800-1859), played as a child on the Common. He was a literary prodigy who is reputed to have written a compendium of world history aged seven. He is best known for the five-volume *History of England.* His nephew and biographer, Sir George Trevelyan, wrote of him that he "used to roam that delightful wilderness of gorse bushes and poplar groves which was to little Tom Macaulay a region of inexhaustible romance and mystery ... exploring the bumpy ground known as the Alps, which no-one above the age of 8 could notice."

13. *William Wilberforce* (1759-1833) *by Sir Thomas Lawrence, 1828*

The Tory member of Parliament for Yorkshire, William Wilberforce (1759-1833) (*right*), who came to Clapham in 1787, conducted a battle against slavery for nearly 50 years, living just long enough to see legislation passed. "Thank God", he wrote four days before his death, "that I have lived to witness a day in which England is prepared to give twenty million sterling for the Abolition of Slavery." He lived and worked on the Battersea Rise side of the Common, next

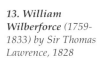

14. *Thomas Babington Macaulay* (1800-1859) *by Sir Francis Grant, 1853*

17

FAMOUS NAMES

IN 1836 SOME local residents formed a committee to obtain leases from the Lords of the Manors in order to preserve and improve the Common, which had become overgrown and unkempt. They raised funds – £7,000 over a 25-year period – for draining and filling up the disused gravel pits and to make a cricket pitch. When there were plans to build a railway across the Common in 1864, 40 subscribers managed to raise funds to block the proposals.

Clapham Common was known for its surrounding "board" houses, or girls' schools. The poet, Percy Bysshe Shelley, as a 19-year-old, roamed over the Common with 16-year-old Harriet Westbrook, a pupil at Miss Hawkes' school, which he referred to as "her prison-house". The couple eloped in

15. Drawing by J. Powell of houses just north of Holy Trinity Church; behind the wrought iron gate was Miss Hawkes' school

1811 and had two children before the marriage collapsed and Shelley went abroad with Mary Godwin, author of *Frankenstein*. In 1816 Harriet drowned herself in the Serpentine.

The Windmill Inn (*above*) has long been a local landmark and Frank Byford, a Clapham diarist, described the annual return from the Derby when the Duke of Wellington, the Prince Consort and the Prime Minister, Lord Palmerston, on horseback, stopped at the Windmill for refreshments.

The Windmill Inn had been an alehouse since the 17th century, and the original mill

16. The Windmill Inn from Frank Byford's diary, written and illustrated in about 1940 recalling his youth in the area in the 1880s

for grinding corn dates back to 1631. In 1848 the Young family acquired the lease, which they own today. This Wandsworth-based, family-owned brewery still delivers to the Windmill by horse-drawn dray.

ONG RD. CLAPHAM COMMON.

GETTING AROUND

I N 1871 THE LEASES obtained by the 1836 Committee from the Lords of the Manors of Battersea and Clapham for the management of the Common expired and in 1874 the local residents passed a resolution stating that they wished the Common to be publicly owned. Both Lords of the Manor haggled over the price, but eventually Earl Spencer of Battersea was paid £10,000 and Colonel Bowyer of Clapham Manor was paid £8,000.

In 1877 Clapham Common was acquired by the Metropolitan Board of Works. Once under public ownership, the Common developed into the green space for recreation and fresh air that it is today. One of the first tasks was to increase the available area for public use; the Board drained about 70 acres of swamp and filled in numerous ditches.

London was growing rapidly and families from miles around would flock to Clapham Common. Transport

17. An electric tram on Long Road, c.1905; horse-drawn trams were replaced by electric trams in 1902

improved during the second half of the 19th century with the railways opening up the suburbs. Trams, first horse-drawn and then electric, linked Clapham with central London and the congested districts close to the Thames. The first tube railway in the world, the City and South London (now

18. Clapham Common Station, opened in 1900 on the corner of Clapham High Street and Clapham Park Rd, opposite its present site

the Northern Line) opened between King William Street and Stockwell in 1890 and was extended to Clapham Common in 1900.

21

TAKING THE AIR

IN THE MID-1880s the Common was evidently a pleasant place for Victorian parents to bring their children on Sundays, perhaps by means of the Clapham Omnibus.

There had been some objections to the "class of people" who flocked to the Common in 1852, after Kennington Common to the east was made into a park and subsequently regularly policed. Worse still, "the keeper employed by the Committee at 23 shillings a week could not keep the whole Common under surveillance nor prevent the gross outrage to females committed in broad daylight."

The treasurer of the committee, whose windows overlooked the Common, insisted that a policeman was needed "constantly among the furze". Prostitutes made their way from Wandsworth Goal

19. Donkey rides on the Common in the 1870s; more than 25 donkeys were available for hire during the summer months

after their release and the outraged treasurer reported scenes that "ought not to be made in a respectable neighbourhood like that."

Contemporary black-and-white photographs, however, show scenes which are the acme of Victorian family respectability.

One of the children who may have enjoyed donkey rides and picnics on the Common was the author of *Eminent Victorians*, the young Lytton Strachey, who was born in March 1880 at Stowey House on South Side. His father, Sir Richard Strachey, an administrator in India for many years, took the house in 1873, renaming it after the village of his family seat in Somerset. Among the literary figures entertained by the Strachey family in Clapham were George Eliot and Robert Browning.

20. A party of children pose for their photograph on the north-eastern part of the Common; in the background is Cock Pond, which later became the paddling pool

A Corner of Clapham Common.

23

THE GROWING COMMUNITY

B Y THE LATE 19TH CENTURY Clapham was becoming built up. "The hand of the speculative builder is heavy, and it effaces old landmarks in the same ruthless fashion as the Goth and Hun swept away the magnificence of Imperial Rome," wrote J. W. Grover in his book *Old Clapham* (1892). Although it takes a loyal resident to liken Clapham to Imperial Rome, it does describe the invasion of the terraced house in to the select community around the Common. Percy Fitzgerald

wrote: "The confectioners on The Pavement have a busy time of it, sending out dinners and equipments in London fashion." The Old Town had become a thriving business centre.

The large estates overlooking the Common also began to give way to terraced villas. John Allnutt's estate – around the area of Elms Road – had been sold off to George Myers as early as 1863 for development for £24,000, although most of the development did not occur until the 1880s.

But as the terraced houses spread in the ensuing decades, there emerged separate communities. The pattern of development repeating itself to the north and west meant that the Common, instead of being peripheral to the Old Town, became a central amenity for a rapidly increasing population.

The bandstand, one of a pair designed by Captain Francis Fowke in 1861 for the Royal Horticultural Society's Garden in South Kensington, was moved to Clapham when the garden was abandoned in 1890.

21. *The drinking fountain, designed by F. Muller of Munich, was first erected in 1884 near London Bridge by the Temperance Society*

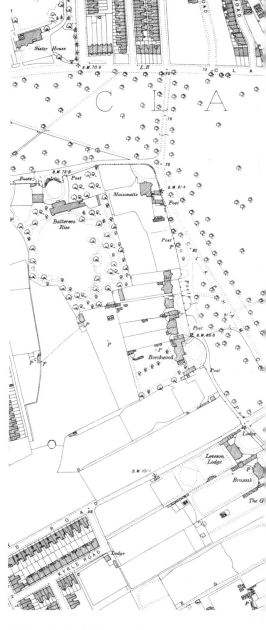

22. *Detail of 1894 Ordance Survey map* showing the gradual development of terraced housing around the Common

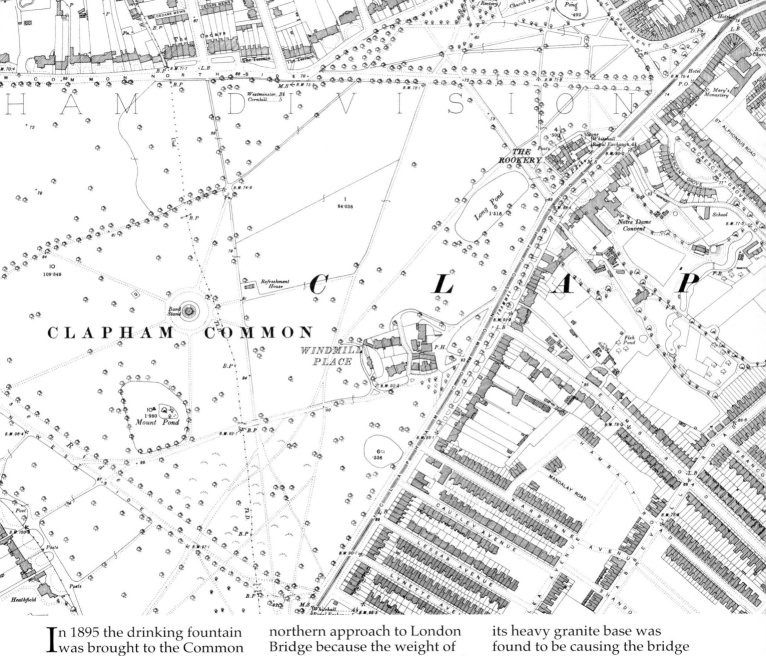

In 1895 the drinking fountain
was brought to the Common
from its original site on the
northern approach to London
Bridge because the weight of
the large bronze sculpture and
its heavy granite base was
found to be causing the bridge
to crack.

25

PASTIMES

CRICKET HAS BEEN PLAYED on the Common since the 18th century and the Clapham Golf Club, formed in 1873, is said to be the second oldest in London. Despite an attempt to ban it in 1895, the club survived – with play allowed only before 9am in the summer and 11am in the winter – until the course was appropriated for use as allotments in 1939. Football, a traditional sport, became even more popular when Clapham Rovers won the FA Cup in 1880.

The advent of photography helped to record for posterity many activities, both formal and informal. Sailing model yachts on the Long Pond, once fenced in by the Lord of the Manor for his own private boating, dates back to the

*23. **Playing tennis** on West Side, not far from the site of the present tennis courts, in the early years of this century*

1870s, making it London's oldest model yachting site. Bathing and boating took place on the Eagle and Mount Ponds and demure ladies in hats and long skirts played tennis. In the cold winters there was skating and tobogganing.

From 1893 onwards money was allocated to improve the green space, raising, levelling and regulating certain parts. There were, however, still complaints, especially when the chestnuts surrounding the area of the former Windmill Pond – the site of the playground today – were cut down and the houses built behind the Windmill Inn.

In 1889 responsibility for the Common passed to the London County Council. In 1913 the German author Leberecht Migge described the Common as a "genuine people's park, an open space for practical use, which had been planned for public requirement." He praised the way ponds had been designated for specific activities and "the layout of the walks which encourage pedestrian traffic."

24. The Common in Winter, c.1910

25. Rowing boats on Eagle Pond in 1910; boating was later transferred to Mount Pond

3608   Clapham Common

END OF AN ERA

T HE COMMON MUST HAVE become less attractive to wildlife with the vast increase in population at the beginning of the 20th century. However, wild flowers, including bog stitchwort, shining crane's bill, milk-wort, common bird's foot and two varieties of St John's wort were still to be found at the turn of the century. "Water-rats, or Voles as some people call them, I have seen myself on Mount Pond island," wrote

26. On 26 August 1913, the sender of this card, who lived off Nightingale Lane, wrote: "This is the path I come across every Sunday evening on my way home from chapel."

Mr Walter Johnson, a local resident with a vast knowledge of plant and bird life. He lists

an astonishing range of birds that he saw or heard on the Common. They include missel thrush, skylark, redwing and fieldfare, willow wren, tawny owl and greenfinch, but, he notes, "redbreast becoming scarce" and "swallows and house martins diminishing in number yearly". The rare chiff-chaff "sing on the Common". Herons were "seen flying over" and the kestrel was "hovering over the Common (once or twice a year)". "The nightingale, not so long ago, was often heard within the vicinity," he wrote sadly.

This rural picture was confirmed by Norman Brind, who lived in Cavendish Road until his death 10 years ago. He remembered, as a small boy, sheep being driven from the Common to a nearby farm, and his father carefully closing the gate to prevent the flowers being eaten. Butchers continued to use the Common for grazing their flocks until the early 1900s.

Carriage horses were regularly watered on the Common and a trough provided by the Metropolitan Drinking Fountain and Cattle Trough Association could still be seen at the corner of Long Road in the 1980s.

27. Sheep grazing *near Mount Pond, c.1908; sheep grazed the Common at least until 1914*

28. The Wilderness, *the north-west part of the Common, was still a place for a secluded picnic*

DIGGING FOR VICTORY

IN BOTH WORLD WARS the Common was totally transformed by the need to turn it over to allotments for food production. Clapham Common had the distinction of being one of the biggest "back to the land" operations in World War I, with 150 people allocated 12 acres within hours of the start of the war. The allotments were along North Side, west of Cedars Road.

King George V and Queen Mary made a tour of South London allotments in July 1918, when prior to their inspection of cabbages at Clapham they visited Wimbledon, where the Queen had been presented with a small pig in a basket covered by a Union Jack.

In World War II allotment holders paid five shillings a year for five-rod plots of land from the London County Council and as the *Clapham News* (8 March 1940) reported, "those who carry their spades and shovels to the Common each weekend include ... officers of the Council, air raid protection wardens, policemen

29. On 20 July 1918, the King and Queen toured allotments in South London; here the King discusses the art of growing prize cabbages

and clerks." Mr John Lamb clearly recalls those allotments "planted right up to the Eagle Pond nearby." The *Clapham News* (18 July 1941) stated that "cabbage and sprouts proudly rear their heads, potatoes grow strongly and onions spring upwards in orderly rows."

Local people have vivid memories of this time. Miss Sylvia Foster has happy memories of picnics on the Common in the summer of 1940 in the shade of the barrage balloons, which were

"like giant grey Dumbos" pegged to the ground in the field near Clapham South Station. She also recalls, painfully, the deep holes dug to disable enemy aircraft landing on the Common. A friend dared her to jump into one of them and she could not get out. Along Rookery Road, pre-fabricated houses were built for emergency housing. These were not removed until the 1950s.

30. During World War II, much of Clapham Common was again turned into allotments to boost food production

ARMING THE COMMON

URING WORLD WAR I part of the Common "was set aside by the War Office ... for the training of officers and men in the use of that deadly weapon – the hand grenade."

On the outbreak of World War II, air-raid shelters were built around the edge of the Common. These were narrow trenches, lined with timber and covered with earth. Inside they only had a narrow wooden bench, as they were intended simply to shelter people during short raids and not as all-night accommodation. An anti-aircraft battery was located in the north-east sector of the Common, consisting of 3.7-in. guns. There were Nissen huts for the gun crews as well as ammunition bunkers, search-lights and sound locators.

Later in the war, deep shelters were built along the route of the Northern Line. The earth from the Clapham South excavations was dumped on the Common, filling in dips and creating low mounds. These shelters, about 100 feet below ground, could each accommodate about 6,000 people, and were fitted with bunks, a canteen and other amenities.

Mrs J. Luck, then a school girl, remembers that the Notre Dame Convent, opposite the Common near the site of the Notre Dame estate, was occupied by the Free French as a recuperation base for the wounded troops. "Their uniforms and berets with the red pompoms became a familiar sight."

32. Meteor Street party on VE Day, 8 May 1945; the bomb shelter extended down at least half the length of the street covering the pavement and part of the road

31. Anti-aircraft guns on the Common in World War II; the 3.7-in. calibre guns are partly sunk into protective emplacements

A local wartime firefighter remembers the Long Pond being used as a water supply for fire fighting. "We even had to use it for fires as far afield as Streatham." From the Hostel of God (now Trinity Hospice) a canteen served the gunners – "so exhausted, they had to empty their tin helmets – they were filled with sweat."

On VE Day throughout the community, there were street parties and the Common itself was the site of the Clapham Victory festival entertainments in 1946. There was open-air dancing by the bandstand. "Although the rain was pouring steadily after lunch ... the audience were there to enjoy themselves."

THE POST-WAR PERIOD

I N THE 1950s the Common was established as a popular place of entertainment. The area – about one-third of the Common – which had been requisitioned by the War Office was finally released in 1948. The remaining earth dumps created by spoil from the deep shelters were removed, and the Common became a temporary coach park during the 1951 Festival of Britain. The deep shelters accommodated sailors on duty at the 1953 Coronation.

Clapham residents crowded on to the Common to hear the concerts on the bandstand. They flocked to the circuses held then – as now – on the ground near The Avenue. The LCC provided a wide-ranging programme of entertainment each summer, including open-air ballet, theatre in a tent, and boxing. The August Bank Holiday in 1954 saw the first of the much-loved horse shows, then a modest gymkhana.

There was a Speaker's Corner on Sunday morning on the area close to Mount Pond which was, according to one resident, "a sort of mini Hyde Park ... and the Communists were decent speakers, civilised, amusing and well read!"

35. A temporary boxing ring set up in 1951

33. The Young's Brewery drays, shire horses with plaited manes and polished brasses, were a popular feature of the annual horse show

34. Classical ballet performed on the grass was one of the many entertainments provided by the LCC during the summer months

THE 1960s

I N 1965 THE Greater London Council, as successor to the London County Council, took over the management of London, including parks and commons. Two years earlier, the Clapham Society had been formed, by a group of residents, as a local amenity society. The Society has a Common Sub-Committee specifically charged to maintain the balance between those who wish to use the sports facilities and children's play facilities on the Common and those interested in a quiet green area in which to observe the wildlife of London.

During the 1960s the range of sports played on the Common increased, as did special events. There were weekly concert parties on the bandstand given by groups with names like the Red Rays and the Joybells, watched by some who paid for deckchairs in the fenced-in enclosure and others who pressed their faces against the railings.

The Festival of Scotland, held every May, included Scottish country dancing and traditional athletic events such

36. Rugby netball, one of the many unusual games enjoyed on the Common, was played every weekday evening in July 1961

37. Women's netball championships were held in 1960 on the netball ground next to the café on Rookery Road

38. The Festival of Scotland in London was held on the Common in May for several years in the 1960s; it included hammer-throwing

as tossing the caber. By now the Horse Show was a three-day event which included sheepdog trials, the Surrey Union Hunt (eventually banned by the GLC) and a children's fancy dress parade. In August, Lambeth library staff held story-telling sessions every afternoon.

THE SPORTING LIFE

S PORTS FLOURISHED ON THE COMMON and by 1975 there were eight tennis courts, five cricket pitches, a putting green, two bowling greens, 19 green and three hard football pitches, a rugby pitch, two hockey pitches and five netball courts. There were also facilities for gaelic football, korfball, rugby netball, horseriding, fishing, model-boat sailing and golf practice as well as the two children's playgrounds and a paddling pool.

There were still concerts, rallies, an open-air chess club (established in the 1930s), children's entertainments and three cafés and a refreshments stall. Something for everyone!

Mount Pond, previously a rowing pond, is now used intensively by anglers. In 1995 a local resident, concerned about injury to birds caused by fishing tackle, led a campaign to ban fishing from the Common. This is still under discussion. Behind the Pond is the Council's most sympathetic landscaping scheme – the Alps –

39. By the 1960s Mount Pond had become the children's rowing pond; small boats coupled together form a type of mini-catamaran

an artificial barrier of low hillocks reducing pollution, noise and visual disturbance from the busy roads. The Alps form an effective barrier

between the sports fields and the seating area. The Council has also introduced lamps and benches in a style consistent with the Victorian bandstand.

40. Long Pond has been used for sailing model yachts since the 1870s; today powered models have joined the fleet

The iron railings around Eagle Pond are particularly praised.

ECOLOGY ON THE COMMON

When the Clapham Society canvassed public opinion in 1975 in *Suggestions for the Future* about possible improvements to the Common, high on the action list was the development of natural resources. This included protecting wildlife, planting shrubs and a wildflower or herb garden near to the bandstand.

In the 1980s the London Wildlife Trust, reflecting increased public awareness of ecology, produced *The Clapham Common Nature Walk*. This booklet noted that there were no longer any amphibians in the ponds "due to lack of aquatic vegetation and competition from fish and fowl." There were, however, leeches, water boatmen and pond skaters in the Eagle and Mount Ponds. Amongst the birds were magpies, carrion crows, creepers, great tits, jays and a pair of kestrels.

Ten years later the London Ecology Unit published *Nature Conservation in Lambeth*. "The woods lack the structure normally associated with wooded habitats in that there are few shrubs and no ground flora species ... the area in between being managed as grasslands." "The flora of the rest of the Common is limited by regular sowing and draining ... the few wildflowers able to withstand the constant trampling include scentless mayweed, common mallow, chickweed, knotweed and groundsel."

On a more positive note, the LEU says: "Within the limits imposed by current resources, the Borough [of Lambeth] is interested in improving the Common as a wildlife site." They note that "a pair of great crested grebes has begun to breed on Mount Pond island for the first time in 1994." The report continues: "Among the trees to be seen are the English oak, beech, sycamore, the plane tree, lime and horse chestnut. In the Nursery Woods there are lombardy poplars and silver birch. In the Battersea Woods the hawthorn and cherry plum planted by the unemployed in the Depression of the 1930s still thrive."

43. A blackbird

44. The heron, drawn here by Christina Bonnett, is often seen on the Common

41. A wild corner of the Common is a popular place for exercising dogs

42. A moorhen

A GREENER SPACE

THE GREAT STORM of October 1987 brought down about 200 mature trees on the Common and over 400 trees needed surgery. There was little interest from the timber trade in the fallen trees, but a local craftsman took some of the wood to make lutes. Another storm in January 1990 had much less effect, partly because the winds were not so strong, but also because the trees were bare of leaves and so offered much less resistance to the wind. The Clapham Society launched a Tree Fund, to which residents gave generously, to replace trees lost in 1987. Sadly, replanting has been insufficient so far to replace the losses.

In the 1980s post and rail fencing was put round all sides of the Common to prevent vehicles parking, without spoiling its appearance.

A Memorial Grove said to have been planted in the early 1990s in memory of the martyred Brazilian rainforest conservationist, Chico Mendes, seems to have disappeared without trace.

*45. **Immense damage** was caused to trees on the Common by the Great Storm of October 1987*

Anglers can find roach, common carp, perch, bream and gudgeon in the Eagle and Mount Ponds. The grey heron visits to help itself to the fish with which the pond is stocked. On one very cold morning in January 1993 a lone drake shoveler was spotted on Eagle Pond – a genuinely wild bird. This is an unusual record for an inner London park.

The new "Alps" behind Mount Pond are now covered with daisies. Children can recapture the joys of their parents' and grandparents' country childhoods – making daisy chains or simply rolling down the banks for fun!

*46. **Anglers on Mount Pond**, with the Alps in the background*

*47. **The central island of Eagle Pond***

THE PEOPLE'S PARK

THE LAST HORSE SHOW was held on the Common in 1985 (it then transferred to Hyde Park) but there are many public entertainments and events still held on the Common, including the Anti-Apartheid concert in 1986 and National Music Day in 1992. The Common is also a convenient starting or finishing point for marches and rallies.

In 1987 the Clapham Society submitted a Code of Practice for the management of such events to Lambeth Council. As a result improved controls have greatly reduced the nuisance to residents. Gospel crusades, fun fairs and circuses continue to be held, although problems do still occur.

Cycle paths, provided as part of a London-wide network of cycle routes, now allow the growing number of cyclists to cross the Common legally, since cycling on the other paths is still against the bye-laws. The 1990's activities of jogging and working-out have reached the Common, and take place happily alongside the more traditional pursuits of dog-walking, kite flying and just sitting around.

49. Feeding the ducks on Mount Pond *although the ducks are now outnumbered by Canada Geese*

50. Evening calm on Mount Pond

48. Cyclists leave Clapham Common at the start of the 1995 London to Brighton cycle ride in aid of the British Heart Foundation

44

THE FUTURE

IT SEEMS A GOOD TIME, 20 years after *Suggestions for the Future,* to re-launch, in time for the millennium, a programme to ensure that the Common is a protected area for wildlife, for relaxation, for sport and for pleasure to benefit all residents, including local schools and their children.

The Story of Clapham Common is a first step. Future prospects are encouraging. At a meeting in July 1995, Lambeth Environmental Services' officials outlined the department's plans. Already London plane trees have been ordered to fill the gaps in The Avenue. The Council intends to create a tree-sponsorship scheme, possibly marking sponsored trees appropriately. The question of repairing the damaged draining system to Long Pond is under discussion, as is more tree planting especially of British broad-leaved varieties, the provision of a garden at the Rookery Road cafe, and the upgrading of sports facilities. The inadequacy of changing rooms and public conveniences for the many sportspeople using the Common is recognised as is the need to create more conservation areas. Inevitably there are conflicts of interest between ecologists who wish to retain dead trees and officials responsible for the safety of the public.

The Council has also recently agreed an outline package of National Lottery bids for submission in the coming year, which is to include infrastructure improvements in parks (that includes the Common). An increase of grant-aid for sport has also been agreed.

These are positive and helpful moves on the part of Lambeth Council. It is vital, therefore, that local residents continue the long-established tradition of interest and concern for the Common, which they have inherited, by working together with Lambeth Council and bodies such as the London Ecology Unit, the London Wildlife Trust and the Clapham Society. Only by doing so can we ensure that future generations will be able to enjoy this oasis of wildlife and green space.

51. Map of Clapham Common *showing the sites and facilities mentioned in the text*

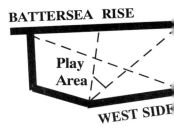

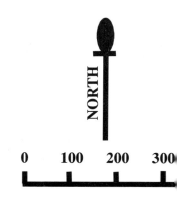

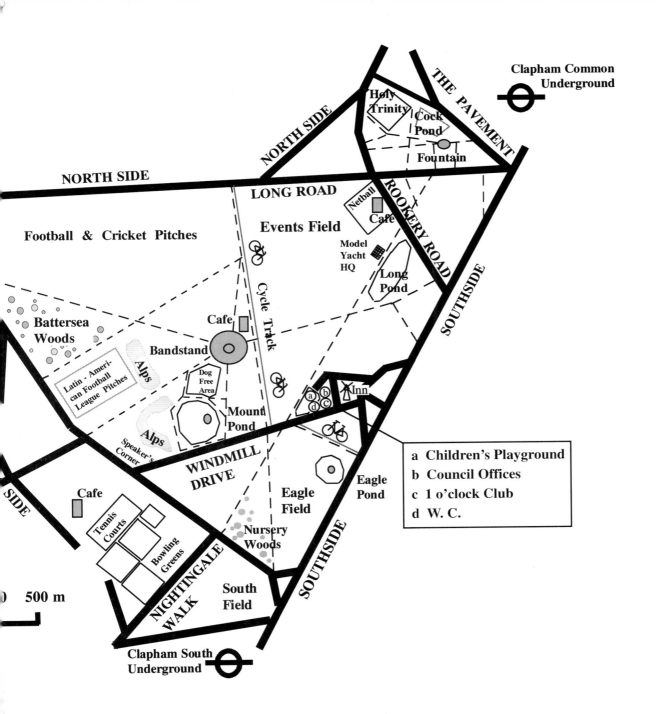

Clapham Common
Underground

Holy Trinity

Cock Pond

Fountain

NORTH SIDE

NORTH SIDE

LONG ROAD

THE PAVEMENT

Events Field

Netball

Cafe

ROOKERY ROAD

Football & Cricket Pitches

Model Yacht HQ

Long Pond

SOUTHSIDE

Cycle Track

Battersea Woods

Cafe

Bandstand

Alps

Latin - American Football League Pitches

Dog Free Area

Inn

a Children's Playground
b Council Offices
c 1 o'clock Club
d W. C.

a b d c

Alps

Speaker's Corner

Mount Pond

WINDMILL DRIVE

Eagle Field

Eagle Pond

SIDE

Cafe

Tennis Courts

Bowling Greens

Nursery Woods

NIGHTINGALE WALK

South Field

SOUTHSIDE

500 m

Clapham South
Underground

ACKNOWLEDGMENTS

The Clapham Society is grateful for much local help with the production of this book. Particular thanks are due to the following:

Simon Adams, who has deftly edited the text; Bernard Battley, who yet again has allowed the Society free access to his unique archive, including the Byford Diary, and has been unfailingly generous with his publishing expertise; Celia Bibby, who helped compile the text and co-ordinate the project; Keith Bibby for the map of the Common on pages 46-47; Christina Bonnett, Outlines, 22 The Pavement, for the specially commissioned watercolour of Clapham Common on the front cover, and the drawings of birds; John Bradbury for advice on local history; Ron Elam, Local Yesterdays (0181-874 8544) for the use of photographs from his large collection of views of South London (copies are available); Fiona Henderson, on whose thesis for the Conservation of Historic Landscapes,

Parks and Gardens Diploma (AA) the text is based; Anthony Shaw of Battersea Local History Library for painstakingly verifying historical details and amplifying some sections; Will Thorpe for designing the book; Charles Williams for reading the text and suggesting improvements; Alyson Wilson for undertaking the picture research and assorted chores; and Neil Wilson, who took the photographs showing the Common in June 1995.

Additional information was generously provided by the Greater London Record Office, London Borough of Lambeth (Parks Office and Press Office), London Ecology Unit and the London Wildlife Trust. Several members of the Clapham Society, including Richard Jones (convener of the Common Sub-Committee), have provided additional help. Sylvia Foster, John Lamb and Joyce Luck have helped to enrich the text with lively reminiscences.

Picture credits
Bernard Battley: 1, 6, 8, 11, 12, 13, 14, 16, 29
Keith Bibby: 51
Christina Bonnett (Outlines): Cover, 42, 43, 44
Pam Cobb: 32
Frederick de Luc: 21
Ron Elam's Local Yesterdays: 17, 20, 23, 24, 25, 26, 27, 28
Greater London Record Office: 33, 34, 35, 36, 37, 38, 39, 40
John How: 45
Illustrated London News: 30
Imperial War Museum: 31
London Transport Museum: 18
Museum of London: 10, 19
Estate of the late Eric Smith: 9, 15
Turner Collection, Tate Gallery: 5
Wandsworth Libraries: 2, 3, 4, 7, 22
Neil Wilson: 41, 46, 47, 48, 49, 50

The Clapham Society
17 Trouville Road
London SW4 8QL

The Story of Clapham Common
was first published in Great Britain in 1995 by
The Clapham Society

Printed in Great Britain by Battley Brothers Limited, 37 Old Town, Clapham, London SW4 0JN

ISBN 0 9500694 3 4